P9-DVD-470

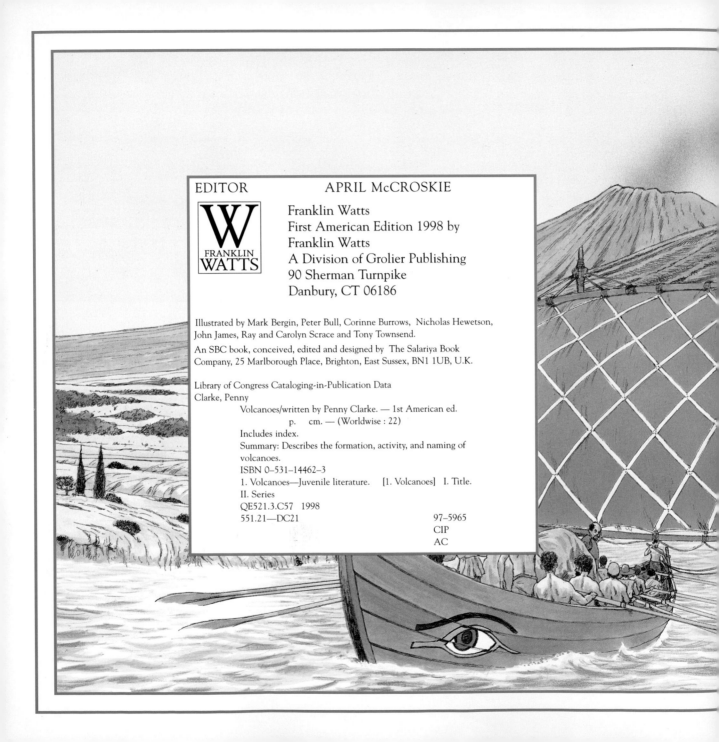

EDITOR   APRIL McCROSKIE

Franklin Watts
First American Edition 1998 by
Franklin Watts
A Division of Grolier Publishing
90 Sherman Turnpike
Danbury, CT 06186

Illustrated by Mark Bergin, Peter Bull, Corinne Burrows, Nicholas Hewetson,
John James, Ray and Carolyn Scrace and Tony Townsend.

An SBC book, conceived, edited and designed by The Salariya Book
Company, 25 Marlborough Place, Brighton, East Sussex, BN1 1UB, U.K.

Library of Congress Cataloging-in-Publication Data
Clarke, Penny
        Volcanoes/written by Penny Clarke. — 1st American ed.
                p.   cm. — (Worldwise : 22)
        Includes index.
        Summary: Describes the formation, activity, and naming of
        volcanoes.
        ISBN 0–531–14462–3
        1. Volcanoes—Juvenile literature.   [1. Volcanoes] I. Title.
        II. Series
        QE521.3.C57 1998
        551.21—DC21   97–5965
                                                             CIP
                                                             AC

volcanoes

Written by
PENNY CLARKE

Series Created & Designed by
DAVID SALARIYA

W
FRANKLIN WATTS
A Division of Grolier Publishing
NEW YORK • LONDON • HONG KONG • SYDNEY
DANBURY, CONNECTICUT

CONTENTS

When volcanoes like Mount St. Helens or Mount Pinatubo erupt most people think of the eruptions as disasters. They *are* disasters for the people whose homes and lives are destroyed. But they are essential because volcanoes are the earth's safety-valves. The pressure within the earth is so great that it would blow apart if the pressure were not released from time to time. Volcanic eruptions release that pressure. They also bring to the surface material from deep within the earth, helping scientists to learn more about our planet.

Pelé is the Hawaiian goddess of fire. Some Hawaiians believe she lives in the volcano Kilauea. Its lava is very runny. When it is thrown into the air it forms long thin strands – like Pelé's hair.

Today we understand why volcanoes erupt, but this knowledge is quite new. For most of human history no one knew why some mountains gave off fire and produced lava. Myths and legends grew to explain the "fire mountains." The word "volcano" comes from such a legend. The ancient Romans believed that Vulcan, their god of fire, had his blacksmith's shop below the Mediterranean island of Vulcano. Its eruptions were a sign that he was working.

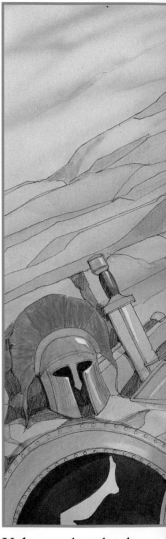

Vulcano, the island after which volcanoes are named, has not had a major eruption since the 19th century.

The Greeks believed Mount Etna in Sicily erupted when Hephaistos, their fire god, was making weapons.

These small black crosses are rock crystals which formed when Mount Vesuvius in southern Italy erupted in 1660. At the time, the people of nearby Naples who found the crystals believed they were signs from God.

The earth is made up of layers.

The crust (the seabed and the ground we walk on) is about 80 kilometres thick. Below are thicker layers. Some consist of rock, others of metal. Some layers are liquid, others are solid. All are very hot. The center, 3822 miles (6370 kilometers) from the surface, is 8132°F (4500°C.)

Scientists do not know exactly how or when the earth was formed. But they believe it probably formed millions of years ago from a huge cloud of dust and gas swirling around the sun.

Crust

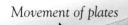

Movement of plates

The earth's surface is made up of plates — huge areas of the land and seabed. Movements deep below the surface make the plates move. Volcanoes occur where the edges of two plates meet.

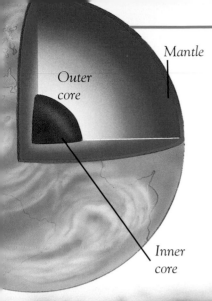

Mantle

Outer core

Inner core

The earth's layers. The mantle is made of white-hot rock. Most volcanoes' lava is from this layer. The outer core is of liquid metal, but the pressure at the earth's center is so great that there the metal is solid.

Magma is the molten rock in a volcano which wells up from deep within the earth. Magma becomes lava or gas when the volcano erupts.

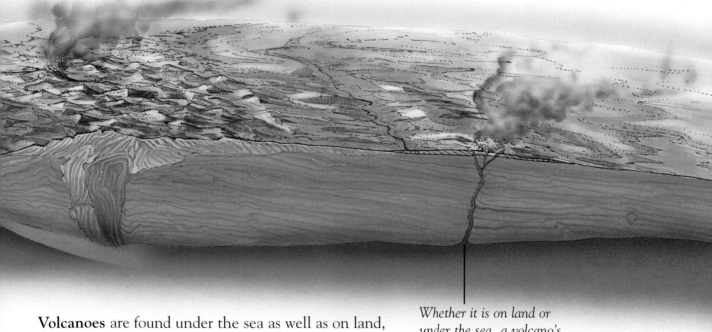

Volcanoes are found under the sea as well as on land, although for centuries no one knew this. As the lava of undersea volcanoes cools on the seabed it hardens and becomes part of the earth's plates.

Whether it is on land or under the sea, a volcano's vent is like a very long chimney reaching deep into the earth.

Without volcanoes the earth would be very different. Around 4000 million years ago the earth was a wilderness of erupting volcanoes. There was little water and no atmosphere (air) for living things to breathe. Scientists now know that all seawater and many gases in the atmosphere came from the first volcanoes and that new eruptions add to what those ancient ones provided.

Areas of volcanic activity change as the earth's surface plates move. This church in eastern France is on the remains of an ancient volcano.

Today, there are about 500 active volcanoes. Most are around the Pacific Ocean, in what is called the "Ring of Fire." Iceland, in the North Atlantic, also has several active volcanoes.

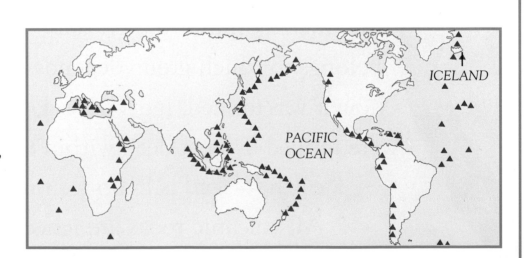

ICELAND

PACIFIC OCEAN

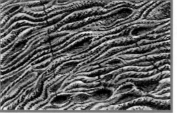

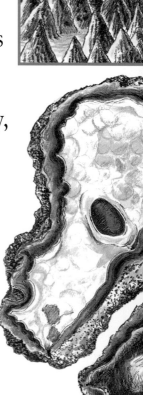

The Giant's Causeway, formed by cooling lava, shows there were once volcanoes in Ireland.

Lava contains gas. The oval shapes in this lava are where bubbles of gas have burst.

Granite, an igneous rock, is cut into blocks for building material.

In Turkey, homes have been cut in eroded lava from Mount Erciyes.

Geology, the
study of rocks, gives clues to the earth's history. Geologists divide rocks into three groups — igneous, sedimentary, and metamorphic. Which rock belongs to which group depends on how it was formed. Igneous rocks were formed by heat deep within the earth — *ignis* is Latin for fire. All volcanic rocks are igneous.

This is an agate — a semi-precious gemstone.

The shape and prints of its bark are the only signs of a tree buried by lava 2000 years ago in Idaho.

This Mexican mountain is eroded (worn away), but the thin vertical lines show it was a volcano.

Crater Lake in Oregon, USA, is so-called because it is in the remains of a once huge volcano.

When gas bubbles in lava burst they leave spaces. Over thousands of years crystals, like this ziolite, form in the spaces.

Agates form in the cavities of cooling volcanic rock.

Diamonds are the hardest natural substance. When cut and polished, they are very valuable.

An uncut diamond embedded in volcanic rock from a diamond mine in South Africa. More diamonds are used in industry than to make jewellery.

Yellow sulphur crystals form as gas in lava cools.

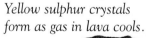

Cut diamonds

15

DIFFERENT TYPES OF VOLCANO

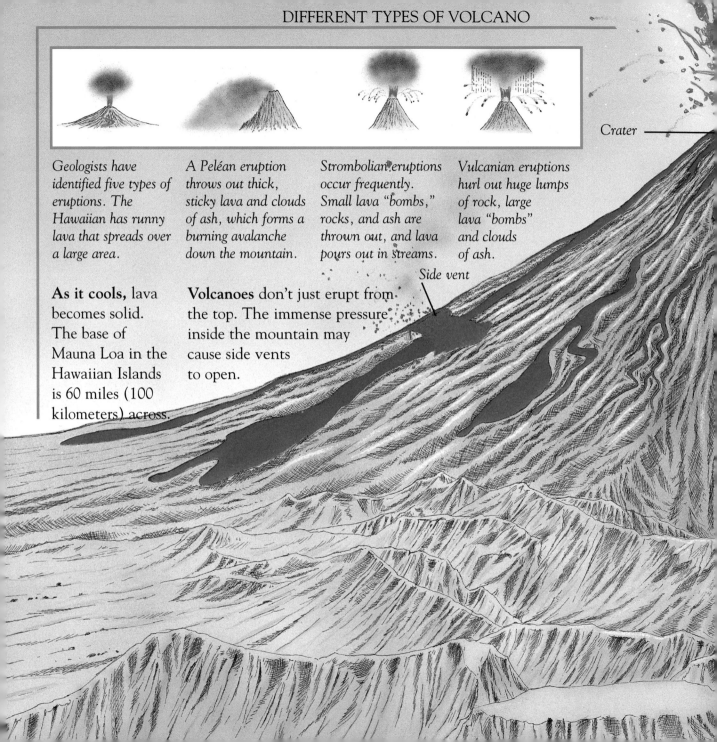

Geologists have identified five types of eruptions. The Hawaiian has runny lava that spreads over a large area.

A Peléan eruption throws out thick, sticky lava and clouds of ash, which forms a burning avalanche down the mountain.

Strombolian eruptions occur frequently. Small lava "bombs," rocks, and ash are thrown out, and lava pours out in streams.

Vulcanian eruptions hurl out huge lumps of rock, large lava "bombs" and clouds of ash.

As it cools, lava becomes solid. The base of Mauna Loa in the Hawaiian Islands is 60 miles (100 kilometers) across.

Volcanoes don't just erupt from the top. The immense pressure inside the mountain may cause side vents to open.

Crater

Side vent

Plinian eruptions are the most explosive. They send ash columns up into the atmosphere.

Central vent

Ash

When a volcano erupts, it gives out gas, water vapor, and lava. Gradually, the lava builds up to form the volcano's cone. But not all lava is the same, so volcanoes vary in shape, from the tall cone of Fujiyama, in Japan, to the low volcanoes on Hawaii.

Fissure (crack)

Sill (magma pool)

Not all magma goes into the volcano's central vent. Some forms pools between layers of rock and solidifies. But if there is a crack in the rock, the magma may erupt far from the vent.

Magma chamber

Mount Rainier in the Cascade Range, USA, (above) *has not erupted in living memory, but it is near Mount St. Helens which erupted in 1980.*

If a volcano has not erupted for centuries will it erupt again? Or is it extinct (dead)? The answer is that no one knows. As the plates of the earth's crust move, areas of volcanic activity change. Scotland had many volcanoes 340 million years ago. Now only some eroded remains are left. Those volcanoes are extinct. But, if a volcano gives off some gas and steam it may erupt again. But no one knows when.

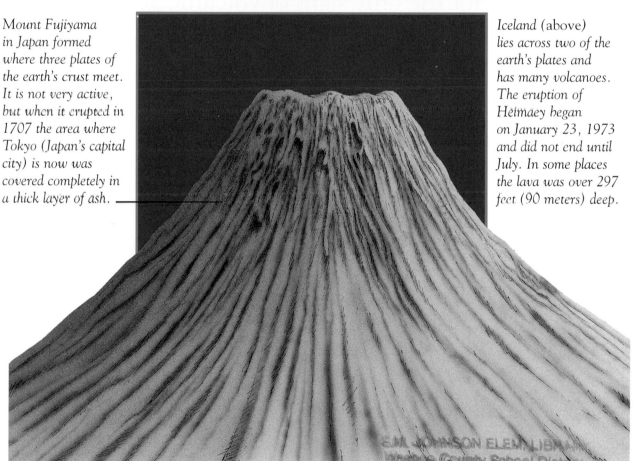

Mount Fujiyama in Japan formed where three plates of the earth's crust meet. It is not very active, but when it erupted in 1707 the area where Tokyo (Japan's capital city) is now was covered completely in a thick layer of ash.

Iceland (above) lies across two of the earth's plates and has many volcanoes. The eruption of Helmaey began on January 23, 1973 and did not end until July. In some places the lava was over 297 feet (90 meters) deep.

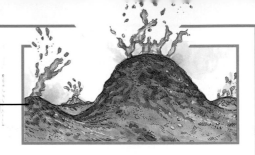

Spatter cones are like big molehills, a yard or so high. They are actually small eruptions of very runny lava.

Erupting volcanoes are

not the only signs of volcanic activity. The magnificent natural fountains, or geysers, of steam and hot water in the U.S.A., Iceland, and New Zealand are all linked to volcanic activity. Other, less dramatic, signs are the bubbling pools of hot, thick volcanic mud which often form near geysers. Smokers are geysers that occur on the seabed, usually where two plates

The geyser at Calistoga, California, can reach 264 feet (80 meters). The warm water is said to cure a medical condition called rheumatism.

At Svartsengi in Iceland heat from the hot springs is used to heat homes. Water from the power plant runs into a pool and is warm enough to swim in – almost as far north as the Arctic Circle.

For thousands of years there has been volcanic activity in Ethiopia, in northeast Africa. The water from spatter cones like this is so salty that over the centuries it has dried and formed vast beds of salt.

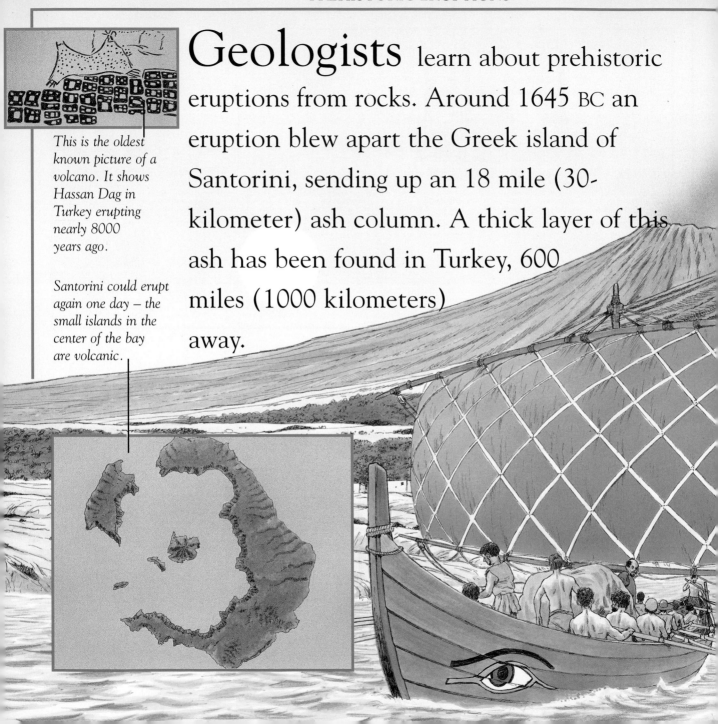

This is the oldest known picture of a volcano. It shows Hassan Dag in Turkey erupting nearly 8000 years ago.

Santorini could erupt again one day – the small islands in the center of the bay are volcanic.

Geologists learn about prehistoric eruptions from rocks. Around 1645 BC an eruption blew apart the Greek island of Santorini, sending up an 18 mile (30-kilometer) ash column. A thick layer of this ash has been found in Turkey, 600 miles (1000 kilometers) away.

The ash cloud from the Santorini eruption was so dense that it lowered temperatures, affecting crops and causing food shortages over a wide area.

The eruption destroyed the rich Minoan civilization on the nearby island of Crete. Thousands died and the magnificent palaces and temples were destroyed.

On August 24,

AD 79, the Roman towns of Herculaneum and Pompeii were destroyed when Vesuvius, a nearby mountain, erupted. Until then no one knew it was a volcano. The historian, Pliny the Younger, saw the eruption. He described how the sun was blotted out as ash fell on the towns and mud-flows devastated the countryside, killing at least 12,000 people.

The volcanic ash and mud that killed the people of Pompeii also preserved their shapes. As it cooled and hardened it formed molds around the bodies.

Eventually the bodies decayed, leaving hollow molds. Today, 18 centuries after the disaster, archaeologists pour plaster into the molds to make casts.

The cast of this victim shows vividly how he struggled to escape the mud and ash.

Scientists have discovered that no seabed rocks are more than 200 million years old — young compared to rocks on land. This suggests the seabed is formed of material from deep within earth, brought up by volcanic eruptions.

Most runny lava is made under the sea. It erupts where the plates of the earth's crust are moving apart. As it cools, it forms part of the plate.

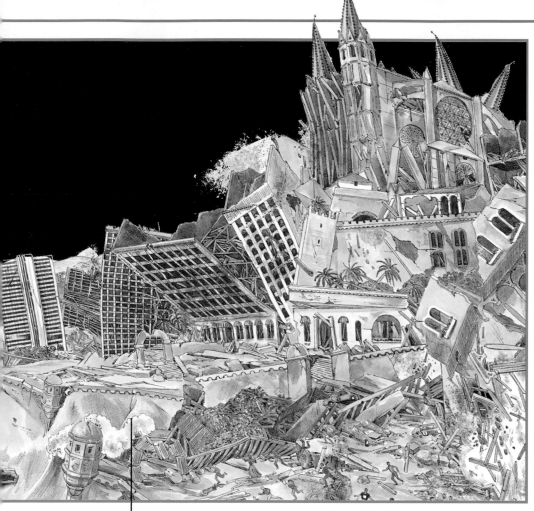

1883 the island
of Krakatoa in
Indonesia was
5.4 miles (9 kilo-
meters) long and
had three
volcanoes.
On August 27,
there were five
explosions.
Hot ash and rock
swept across the
island and out into
the sea, causing
tsunamis up to 132
feet (40 meters)
high. Around 3.6
miles (6 kilo-
meters) of the
island disappeared,
36,000 people died
and 165 villages
were destroyed.

*Tsunami means
"over-flowing wave"
in Japanese.
A 280 feet
(85 meters) high
tsunami hit Ishigaki,
Japan, in 1971,
hurling a 750-ton
rock 1.5 miles
(2.5 kilometers).*

Undersea eruptions can cause as much damage as those on land. They may trigger tsunamis, huge waves, which can travel at 480 miles (800 kilometers) per hour.

Ash from Mount St. Helens fell in the Columbia River. On May 18 the river was 39.6 feet (12 meters) deep and full of ocean-going ships. By 5A.M. next morning it was 13.2 feet (4 meters) deep and the ships were stuck.

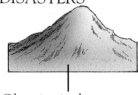

Gleaming in the sunshine, the mountain gives no clue to the forces building up inside.

Until April 1980 Mount St. Helens was popular with tourists. But as the warnings of an eruption increased the authorities cleared the area.

The blast caused by the explosion devastated an area 12 miles (20 kilometers) by 18 miles (30 kilometers). Trees once 148.5 feet (45 meters) tall lay like straw.

The force of the explosion was so great it blew off the top 1320 feet (400 meters) of the mountain.

This is the same view as the picture above, but four months after the eruption. The first grass has started to grow but it will be years before there are big trees again.

Some volcanoes give warnings of an eruption. On March 20, 1980, an earthquake occurred 19.2 miles (32 kilometers) from Mount St. Helens in Washington State, USA. Others followed. On March 27, an ash column rose 23,100 feet (7000 meters) into the air after an explosion. More explosions followed. Then, on May 18, the eruption came. This time the ash column was 15 miles (25 kilometers) high.

Bare hillsides

Tree stump

Mount Vesuvius has erupted often since AD 79. In 1631, over 495 feet (150 meters) of rock were blown from the summit.

Vesuvius' last major exlosion was in 1944, when it damaged a US air base during the Second World War.

With the tourists came guidebooks. One, written in 1883, advised everyone to wear their oldest clothes because of the rough ground. It warned that colored dresses would be stained by the sulphur fumes, and even strong boots would be cut by the sharp lava.

The clothes worn by 19th-century tourists, especially women, made climbing volcanoes rather difficult.

Like volcanic eruptions, tourists cause damage. Most of those going to Vesuvius also visit Pompeii, which is being eroded by their feet!

As well as guidebooks, tourists like souvenirs. At Vesuvius, probably the world's most visited volcano, lumps of lava are popular.

The author of another guidebook warned tourists about hiring guides, declaring that they were all ignorant. The author was clearly trying to make the point that his book was a better guide!

During the 18th and 19th centuries, rich people from northern Europe made a "Grand Tour" of Italy, and sometimes Greece and Egypt, too. These early tourists went to see archaeological sites, important buildings and the art of the countries they visited. Vesuvius was particularly popular because there was nothing like it farther north. People did not realize that many of their own countries, France, Ireland, and Britain, for example, once had active volcanoes. Modern tourists still visit volcanoes — Montserrat in the Caribbean promotes its volcano as a tourist attraction.

From 1890 to 1944, a funicular railway took tourists up to the crater of Vesuvius. Today you can still go up to the crater — but on foot.

Vulcanologists are

scientists who study volcanoes. They try to predict when a volcano will erupt. This is very difficult, especially if a volcano has been dormant (quiet) for centuries. But there are clues. Tiltmeters on a volcano's side record changes in the mountain's slope, suggesting activity inside. Or, the volcano might begin to give off more ash and gas.

Studying volcanoes is dangerous work, even with protective clothing. The metal coating on this suit reflects the heat of an eruption, keeping the wearer cool.

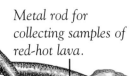

Metal rod for collecting samples of red-hot lava.

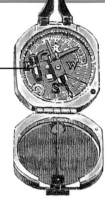

Vulcanologists need to record an erupting volcano's changing shape quickly. They use a combined spirit level (which measures the horizontal) and compass to do this.

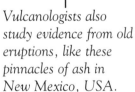

Vulcanologists also study evidence from old eruptions, like these pinnacles of ash in New Mexico, USA.

Mount Etna in Sicily is a good volcano to study because it is constantly but mildly active. But scientists still face temperatures of 1832°F (1000°C).

Where volcanoes continue to erupt there is no plant or animal life.

Wind and rain gradually break down the lava on the upper slopes of volcanoes.

Lava particles are washed down into the valleys by the heavy tropical rain.

Lichens are the first living organisms to grow on lava.

A well-established lichen provides shelter for tiny organisms.

A major volcanic eruption devastates the area around it. But, as scientists learned after the eruption of Mount St. Helens, life returns to the land amazingly quickly.

Gas from erupting volcanoes often contains poisonous chemicals.

The erosion of lava and the regrowth of plants is fastest in warm wet places like Hawaii.

In Hawaii's lush valleys live many unique species, including the Hawaiian goose.

Moss follows the growth of lichens on the lava as it slowly breaks down.

The Hawaiian Islands have a long history of volcanic activity. But because volcanic rock eventually breaks down to form a rich soil, they also have a wonderful variety of plants and animals.

Eventually the soil will be thick enough for large plants and trees.

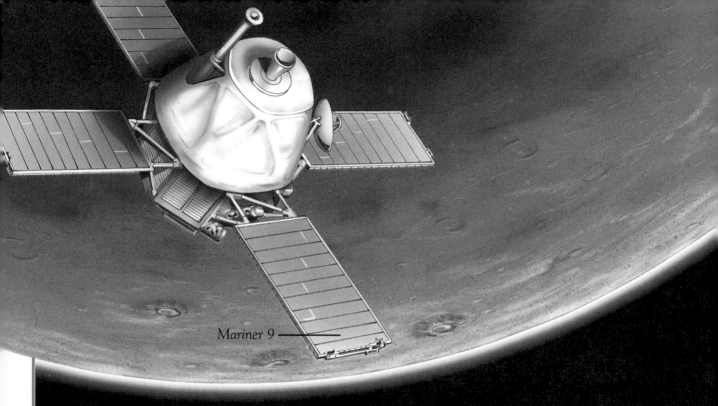

Mariner 9

Satellites and other space probes have shown that earth is not the only place where there are volcanoes. Because most of the planets are too far away and not suitable for human life, most of the information is collected by computer and radioed back to earth.

The satellite *Mariner 9* was launched on its flight to Mars on May 30, 1971. After 167 days the satellite reached the planet and started transmitting pictures. These showed that Mars has many volcanoes.

Some of the volcanoes on Mars are massive. Olympus Mons, is 15 miles (25 kilometers) high and 324 miles (540 kilometers) wide. In contrast, Mount Everest, the highest mountain on earth, is less than 5.4 miles (9 kilometers) high and Mauna Kea, Hawaii, is a little over 6 miles (10 kilometers) from its base on the seabed to its peak, while the Grand Canyon is only 17.4 miles (29 kilometers) wide.

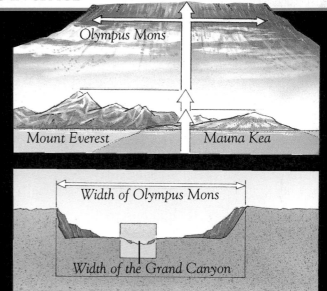

Olympus Mons

Mount Everest

Mauna Kea

Width of Olympus Mons

Width of the Grand Canyon

There are also volcanoes on the moon. Scientists know that earthquakes occur there, but do not know if any of the volcanoes are still active. Basalt is a volcanic rock, and astronauts collected basalt rocks during the moon landings – proof of past eruptions.

An eruption on Io, a small moon that orbits the planet Jupiter – one of many signs of volcanic activity on Io.

USEFUL WORDS

Core Earth's inner layer.

Crater Mouth of a volcano.

Crust Earth's outer layer.

Dormant A volcano that has not erupted for a long time, but which still shows signs of activity, such as geysers and earth tremors.

Eroded Worn away.

Extinct A volcano that cannot erupt any more because its vent no longer reaches magma.

Geyser A natural fountain of hot water; a sign of volcanic activity.

Igneous rock Rock formed by the earth's intense heat.

Lava Molten material which flows from a volcano when it erupts. Runny lava can flow at speeds of up to 90 miles (50 kilo-meters) per hour.

Magma The molten material in a volcano.

Mantle The layer of the earth between the crust and the core.

Metamorphic rock Sedimentary rock altered by heat and pressure deep in the earth.

Molten Made liquid by heat.

"Ring of Fire" Area around the Pacific Ocean with many active volcanoes.

Sedimentary rock Type of rock formed by the erosion of igneous rock.

Vent Passage in a volcano through which magma reaches the earth's surface.

INDEX

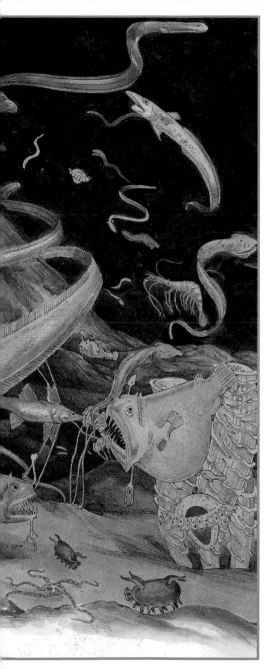